4○minute
BIBLE STUDIES

Key Principles of Biblical Fasting

Kay Arthur & Pete De Lacy

PRECEPT MINISTRIES INTERNATIONAL

WATERBROOK
PRESS

KEY PRINCIPLES OF BIBLICAL FASTING
PUBLISHED BY WATERBROOK PRESS
12265 Oracle Boulevard, Suite 200
Colorado Springs, Colorado 80921

All Scripture quotations are taken from the New American Standard Bible® (NASB).
© Copyright The Lockman Foundation 1960, 1962, 1963, 1968, 1971, 1972, 1973,
1975, 1977, 1995. Used by permission. (www.Lockman.org).

Italics in Scripture quotations reflect the author's added emphasis.

ISBN 978-0-307-45765-3

Published in the United States by WaterBrook Multnomah, an imprint of the Crown
Publishing Group, a division of Random House Inc., New York.

WATERBROOK and its deer colophon are registered trademarks of Random House Inc.

Printed in the United States of America
2012

10 9 8 7 6 5

SPECIAL SALES
Most WaterBrook Multnomah books are available at special quantity discounts when
purchased in bulk by corporations, organizations, and special-interest groups. Custom
imprinting or excerpting can also be done to fit special needs. For information, please
e-mail SpecialMarkets@WaterBrookMultnomah.com or call 1-800-603-7051.

CONTENTS

HOW TO USE THIS STUDY

This small-group study is for people who are interested in learning for themselves more about what the Bible says on various subjects, but who have only limited time to meet together. It's ideal, for example, for a lunch group at work, an early morning men's group, a young mothers' group meeting in a home, a Sunday-school class, or even family devotions. (It's also ideal for small groups that typically have longer meeting times—such as evening groups or Saturday morning groups—but want to devote only a portion of their time together to actual study, while reserving the rest for prayer, fellowship, or other activities.)

This book is designed so that all the group's participants will complete each lesson's study activities *at the same time*. Discussing your insights drawn from what God says about the subject reveals exciting, life-impacting truths.

Although it's a group study, you'll need a facilitator to lead the study and keep the discussion moving. (This person's function is *not* that of a lecturer or teacher. However, when this book is used in a Sunday-school class or similar setting, the teacher should feel free to lead more directly and to bring in other insights in addition to those provided in each week's lesson.)

If *you* are your group's facilitator, the leader, here are some helpful points for making your job easier:

- Go through the lesson and mark the text before you lead the group. This will give you increased familiarity with the material and will enable you to facilitate the group with greater ease. It may be easier for you to lead the group through the instructions for marking if you, as a leader, choose a specific color for each symbol you mark.

- As you lead the group, start at the beginning of the text and simply read it aloud in the order it appears in the lesson, including the "insight boxes," which appear throughout. Work through the lesson together, observing and discussing what you learn. As you read the Scripture verses, have the group say aloud the word they are marking in the text.

- The discussion questions are there simply to help you cover the material. As the class moves into the discussion, many times you will find that they will cover the questions on their own. Remember, the discussion questions are there to guide the group through the topic, not to squelch discussion.

- Remember how important it is for people to verbalize their answers and discoveries. This greatly strengthens their personal understanding of each week's lesson. Try to ensure that everyone has plenty of opportunity to contribute to each week's discussions.

- Keep the discussion moving. This may mean spending more time on some parts of the study than on others. If necessary, you should feel free to spread out a lesson over more than one session. However, remember that you don't want to slow the pace too much. It's much better to leave everyone "wanting more" than to have people dropping out because of declining interest.

- If the validity or accuracy of some of the answers seems questionable, you can gently and cheerfully remind the group to stay focused on the truth of the Scriptures. Your object is to learn what the Bible says, not to engage in human philosophy. Simply stick with the Scriptures and give God the opportunity to speak. His Word *is* truth (John 17:17)!

KEY PRINCIPLES OF BIBLICAL FASTING

Do you long for intimacy with God? Do you desire to feel His presence, to hear His voice, to sense His pleasure? If drawing near to God is the desire of your heart, then we invite you to join us in an invigorating study of the discipline of fasting.

Since ancient times, fasting has been considered an essential means of deepening one's faith and connection with God. But in recent years it has become an increasingly rare—and often misunderstood—practice. Many wonder if fasting is an outmoded form of spiritual discipline, something modern-day Christians needn't bother with. Others are convinced this discipline is only for the superspiritual. And some see it only as a bizarre ritual connected to other faiths.

The Bible refers to fasting more than fifty times, and in this six-week study we'll examine many of those passages to learn what the Word of God teaches about the topic. We'll consider what fasting involves and what it means to the average Christian. As you discover for yourself the biblical principles behind this practice and observe its impact on the lives of the faithful throughout history, you'll discover the unique role fasting plays in the life of the church. And by the end of our time together, you'll be equipped to decide how you will enter into the discipline of fasting as a means of deepening your walk with God.

Let's start our study of fasting by examining what Jesus said on the subject in His Sermon on the Mount. Then we'll look at some Old Testament references to this practice to see what we can learn about its nature and purpose.

OBSERVE

The Sermon on the Mount records Jesus' teaching about the basics of righteous living. Let's look specifically at what He said about fasting.

Leader: *Read Matthew 6:1, 16–18 aloud. As you read, have the group say aloud and...*

- *underline every occurrence of **whenever** or **when you.***
- *circle every reference to* (**fasting.**)

As you read the text, it's helpful to have the group say the key words aloud as they mark them. This way everyone will be sure to mark every occurrence of the word, including any synonymous words or phrases. Do this throughout the study.

MATTHEW 6:1, 16–18

1 Beware of practicing your righteousness before men to be noticed by them; otherwise you have no reward with your Father who is in heaven....

16 Whenever you fast, do not put on a gloomy face as the hypocrites do, for they neglect their appearance so that they will be noticed by men when they are fasting. Truly I say to you, they have their reward in full.

17 But you, when you fast, anoint your head and wash your face

18 so that your fasting will not be noticed by men, but by your Father who is in secret; and your Father who sees what is done in secret will reward you.

INSIGHT

The word *fast* in this passage is translated from the Greek word *nesteuo*, which means "to abstain from food or drink."

DISCUSS

• What did you learn from marking *whenever* and *when you*? *it seems to be something practiced not an if you fast & can be done anytime*

• What did you learn from marking the references to fasting? *Dont put on gloomy face hypocrids do this to be notices by men Anoint head wash face Fast so as not to be noticed*

• From what you read in this passage, did Jesus seem to expect His listeners to fast? Explain your answer. *Absolutely. He said when you fast not to*

• If you've ever fasted, describe your experience. What prompted you to fast and what was the outcome? *Cravings weak Tempted to break headaches - physical clanty when reading word Fasted for specific answers*

OBSERVE

We've seen what Jesus expected of His followers when it came to fasting, but did He ever observe this practice Himself? *yes*

Leader: Read aloud Matthew 4:1–4 and have the group…

- *mark each reference to **Jesus,** including pronouns, with a cross:* †
- *circle the word **fasted.***

DISCUSS

- What did you learn from marking the references to Jesus?

*Led by Spirit into the wildernes
Tempted by Devil to turn Stones to bread
Fasted 40 days + nights
Hungry
He responded w/ the word of God*

- What does this passage reveal about His perspective on fasting?

*That He relied on the Spirit
That it is necessary for life*

MATTHEW 4:1–4

1 Then Jesus was led up by the Spirit into the wilderness to be tempted by the devil.

2 And after He had fasted forty days and forty nights, He then became hungry.

3 And the tempter came and said to Him, "If You are the Son of God, command that these stones become bread."

4 But He answered and said, "It is written, 'Man shall not live on bread alone, but on every word that proceeds out of the mouth of God.'"

ISAIAH 58:1–3A

¹ Cry loudly, do not hold back; raise your voice like a trumpet, and declare to My people their transgression and to the house of Jacob their sins.

² Yet they seek Me day by day and delight to know My ways, as a nation that has done righteousness and has not forsaken the ordinance of their God. They ask Me for just decisions, they delight in the nearness of God.

³ᴬ "Why have we fasted and You do not see? Why have we humbled ourselves and You do not notice?"

OBSERVE

Now let's go to Isaiah 58, the most comprehensive passage about fasting in the Bible. This message originally was given to God's people, the Jews, yet we know from Romans 15:4 that "whatever was written in earlier times was written for our instruction."

The context for this passage is that God's people had been fasting in the wrong spirit. Though they outwardly seemed sincere, God knew their hearts and saw through their attempts to manipulate Him.

Leader: Read Isaiah 58:1–3a aloud. As you read, have the group…

- *underline all references to **My people,** including pronouns and synonyms such as **the house of Jacob.***
- *circle the word **fasted.***

INSIGHT

The word *fasted* in this passage is translated from the Hebrew word *tsum,* which means "abstained from food." The only fast God required of His people occurred each year on the Day of Atonement, Yom Kippur. However, fasting was practiced in a variety of circumstances as a means of seeking God's help.

The word *humbled,* translated from the Hebrew word *anah,* refers here to self-afflicted contrition or bowing down.

DISCUSS

• What did God tell Isaiah to do in verse 1?

To cry loudly to the people of Israel + declare their transgressions + sins

• What did you learn from marking the references to God's people? What was happening with them? They were transgressing & sinning. They were seeking God acting like a nation who had done righteousness but Abby were concerned God was not answering

- In verse 3, what action is described as a parallel to fasting?

  Humbling oneself

- God's people looked sincere and eager; however, would He call what they were doing sin if they were truly sincere? Explain your answer.

  To the outsider it looked real. To God who saw the heart I knew it was not Sincere

- The people went to the temple, obeyed God's laws, fasted, and appeared eager to seek the Lord; but their worship was only an outward show. What does that tell us about the condition of their hearts?

  Did not match the action

- From what you have seen, is God more concerned about our outward appearance or the condition of our heart?

  The condition of my heart

OBSERVE

Let's continue observing Isaiah 58.

Leader: Read Isaiah 58:3b–5 aloud and have the group...

- *underline the words **you** and **your**.*
- *circle each occurrence of the word **fast.***

DISCUSS

- How did God describe the way Israel was fasting?

- What kind of practices did Israel engage in when fasting, according to verse 3?

  Pursuing their desires & driving their workers hard

- What did God admonish the people about in verse 4? Were they truly humble as they claimed earlier? Explain your answer.

- Did God find Israel's *outward* practices acceptable? Why or why not?

- According to what you've read, is the external ritual of fasting enough to be heard by God? Explain your answer.

ISAIAH 58:3B–5

3B Behold, on the day of your fast you find your desire, and drive hard all your workers.

4 Behold, you fast for contention and strife and to strike with a wicked fist. You do not fast like you do today to make your voice heard on high.

5 Is it a fast like this which I choose, a day for a man to humble himself? Is it for bowing one's head like a reed and for spreading out sackcloth and ashes as a bed? Will you call this a fast, even an acceptable day to the LORD?

ISAIAH 58:6–12

6 Is this not the fast which I choose, to loosen the bonds of wickedness, to undo the bands of the yoke, and to let the oppressed go free and break every yoke?

7 Is it not to divide your bread with the hungry and bring the homeless poor into the house; when you see the naked, to cover him; and not to hide yourself from your own flesh?

8 Then your light will break out like the dawn, and your recovery will speedily spring forth; and your righteousness will go before you; the glory of the LORD will be your rear guard.

OBSERVE

Let's listen as the Lord continues speaking in Isaiah 58.

Leader: *Read aloud Isaiah 58:6–12 and have the group do the following:*

- *circle every reference to **fasting.***
- *mark every reference to **the Lord**, including pronouns, with a triangle:*
- *underline every reference to **Israel**, including pronouns such as **you, your,** and **yourself.***

DISCUSS

- What did God tell Israel was the right kind of fast? What would be the result of such a fast?

• Contrast this with Isaiah 58:3b–5. Which kind of fasting reveals a heart truly concerned with spiritual matters? Explain your answer.

⁹ Then you will call, and the LORD will answer; you will cry, and He will say, "Here I am." If you remove the yoke from your midst, the pointing of the finger and speaking wickedness,

¹⁰ And if you give yourself to the hungry and satisfy the desire of the afflicted, then your light will rise in darkness and your gloom will become like midday.

¹¹ And the LORD will continually guide you, and satisfy your desire in scorched places, and give strength to your bones; and you will be like a watered garden, and like a spring of water whose waters do not fail.

12 Those from among you will rebuild the ancient ruins; you will raise up the age-old foundations; and you will be called the repairer of the breach, the restorer of the streets in which to dwell.

ISAIAH 58:13–14

13 If because of the sabbath, you turn your foot from doing your own pleasure on My holy day, and call the sabbath a delight, the holy day of the LORD honorable, and honor it, desisting from your own ways, from seeking your own pleasure and speaking your own word,

14 Then you will take delight in the LORD,

• What did God promise to do if Israel would fast according to His desires?

OBSERVE

The keeping of the Sabbath was a barometer of one's faithfulness to the Mosaic covenant. A person who observed the Sabbath according to the Law was acknowledging his dependence on God by seeking Him above his own desires.

Leader: Read Isaiah 58:13–14 aloud and have the group do the following:

- *double underline every reference to* **the Sabbath,** *including any pronouns and the synonym* **holy day.**
- *underline every reference to* **Israel,** *including the pronouns* **you** *and* **your** *as before.*
- *mark with a triangle each reference to* **the Lord,** *including pronouns.*

INSIGHT

Exodus 20:11 says, "For in six days the LORD made the heavens and the earth, the sea and all that is in them, and rested on the seventh day; therefore the LORD blessed the sabbath day and made it holy." The seventh day of the week was to be kept as a "sabbath to the LORD" (Exodus 20:8–11). On that day no one, including servants and visitors, was to work.

and I will make you ride on the heights of the earth; and I will feed you with the heritage of Jacob your father, for the mouth of the LORD has spoken.

DISCUSS

• What did the people of Israel need to do in order to please God in the way they kept the Sabbath?

• What would God do for Israel if the people observed the Sabbath with a right attitude?

• In these verses about keeping the Sabbath, what similarities do you find related to the previous passages about Israel's behavior and attitude toward fasting?

• Discuss what principles, if any, you can discern from these passages regarding God's response to a person's attitude or heart.

OBSERVE

Because of the depraved state of the nation, God would have to initiate salvation. Again God spoke of the people's sin and how it was preventing Him from saving them.

Leader: Read Isaiah 59:1–2 aloud and have the group…
- *mark every reference to **the Lord,** including synonyms and pronouns, with a triangle.*
- *underline each occurrence of the words **you** and **your.***

DISCUSS

- What did you learn from marking *you* and *your?*

- What did you learn from marking the references to the Lord?

- What point was the Lord making? Is it that He *cannot* hear or save?

- From all we have seen in this lesson, what have you learned about fasting?

ISAIAH 59:1–2

¹ Behold, the LORD's hand is not so short that it cannot save; nor is His ear so dull that it cannot hear.

² But your iniquities have made a separation between you and your God, and your sins have hidden His face from you so that He does not hear.

WRAP IT UP

What does it take to be close to God and hear from Him? We saw that Jesus expected fasting to be a regular part of His followers' lives, something that would be rewarded by God. In addition He Himself fasted in the wilderness.

The people of Israel thought they could be right with God simply by performing the ritual of fasting. But they didn't hear from God, and they didn't understand why.

The answer was sin! Sin had separated them from God so that He *would* not listen to their cry. God was concerned with their motives as well as their behavior. Fasting would have no effect until they dealt with their sin.

The perspective of eternal God has not changed since the days of Isaiah. He wants us to obey from our hearts, not merely follow a ritual. If we are living in disobedience, then fasting won't draw us close to God. He won't listen. It's not that God *can't* hear, but that He *chooses* not to listen to the cry of the unrepentant sinner.

What is your response to this warning from God? Will you respond by saying, "I'm okay. The Lord knows my heart." Or will you fast, examining your heart and your ways to see if there be any way in you that is displeasing to the Lord (Psalm 139:23–24)?

If you truly want to draw closer to God, you'll find you can only connect with Him according to His Word.

We saw in Isaiah last week that fasting is intended to make your heart right with the Lord as you examine your life and repent of sin. We also saw that outward religious rituals are not enough to bring us close to God. The example of Israel showed that fasting alone, when it is performed as a ritual, doesn't sanctify anyone.

These days we don't hear many calls to fast, nor is fasting a common practice. Is this because we don't recognize our sin? This week, let's explore further the relationship between fasting and sin.

OBSERVE

Soon after God led the Israelites out of Egypt, they chose sin over righteousness. Let's read what Moses said about these events forty years later as he reminded the people of their behavior and its effect on their relationship with God.

Leader: *Read Deuteronomy 9:9–19 aloud. Have the group do the following:*
- *draw a box around each reference to **Moses**, including pronouns:* ☐
- *underline each reference to **the Israelites**, including synonyms such as **your people** and pronouns such as **you, yourselves, they,** and **them**.*

DEUTERONOMY 9:9–19

9 When I went up to the mountain to receive the tablets of stone, the tablets of the covenant which the LORD had made with you, then I remained on the mountain forty days and nights; I neither ate bread nor drank water.

10 The LORD gave me the two tablets of stone written by the finger of God; and on

them were all the words which the LORD had spoken with you at the mountain from the midst of the fire on the day of the assembly.

11 It came about at the end of forty days and nights that the LORD gave me the two tablets of stone, the tablets of the covenant.

12 Then the LORD said to me, "Arise, go down from here quickly, for your people whom you brought out of Egypt have acted corruptly. They have quickly turned aside from the way which I commanded them; they have made a molten image for themselves."

• *circle every reference to* (fasting.) *Watch carefully for synonymous references to* **not eating food or drinking water.**

DISCUSS

• What did you learn from marking the references to Moses?

• According to verse 14, what did the Lord consider doing to the people? What offer did He make to Moses?

• What had provoked God to such anger?

13 The LORD spoke further to me, saying, "I have seen this people, and indeed, it is a stubborn people.

14 "Let Me alone, that I may destroy them and blot out their name from under heaven; and I will make of you a nation mightier and greater than they."

• How many times did Moses fast in this passage, and for how long? Describe the circumstances surrounding each fast.

15 So I turned and came down from the mountain while the mountain was burning with fire, and the two tablets of the covenant were in my two hands.

16 And I saw that you had indeed sinned against the LORD your God. You had made for yourselves a molten calf; you had turned aside quickly from the way which the LORD had commanded you.

17 I took hold of the two tablets and threw them from my hands and smashed them before your eyes.

18 I fell down before the LORD, as at the first, forty days and nights; I neither ate bread nor drank water, because of all your sin which you had committed in doing what was evil in the sight of the LORD to provoke Him to anger.

19 For I was afraid of the anger and hot displeasure with which the LORD was wrathful against you in order to destroy you, but the LORD listened to me that time also.

• What was Moses' motivation in fasting?

• What principles, if any, do you find here for our times and our nation?

OBSERVE

Like Moses, Samuel was chosen by God to lead His people. The passage you're about to read took place in a time when Israel was suffering at the hands of her long-time enemies, the Philistines.

Leader: Read 1 Samuel 7:3–6 aloud. As you read, have the group…
- *underline every reference to **the house of Israel,** including synonyms such as **sons of Israel** and pronouns such as **you** and **your.***
- *circle the word **fasted.***

INSIGHT
Baal, which means "lord, owner, possessor, or husband," was the Canaanite god of fertility.
Ashtaroth was the Canaanite goddess of fertility, love, and war. According to Greek mythology, she was the wife of Baal.

1 SAMUEL 7:3–6

3 Then Samuel spoke to all the house of Israel, saying, "If you return to the LORD with all your heart, remove the foreign gods and the Ashtaroth from among you and direct your hearts to the LORD and serve Him alone; and He will deliver you from the hand of the Philistines."

4 So the sons of Israel removed the Baals and the Ashtaroth and served the LORD alone.

5 Then Samuel said, "Gather all Israel to Mizpah and I will pray to the LORD for you."

6 They gathered to Mizpah, and drew water and poured it out before the LORD, and fasted on that day and said there, "We have sinned against the LORD." And Samuel judged the sons of Israel at Mizpah.

DISCUSS

• What was Samuel calling Israel to do, and why?

• How did the people respond?

• What did Samuel promise to do for the people?

• What did the Israelites do at Mizpah related to their sin?

• Compare the motivation behind the Israelites' fasting at Mizpah with Moses' motivation for fasting in Deuteronomy 9. What similarities or differences do you observe?

OBSERVE

Sixty-six years after the kingdom of Judah was defeated and her people taken to Babylon, the Medo-Persians, under the rule of Darius, overthrew the Babylonian kingdom. The Jewish exile Daniel searched the Scriptures in order to understand the events of which he was a vital part, having revealed God's imminent judgment to the Babylonian king Belshazzar. Daniel realized that Jeremiah had predicted Israel would be in Babylon for seventy years, and thus he understood that Darius's victory meant the end of their captivity was near.

Leader: Read Daniel 9:1–5 aloud. Have the group do the following:

- *draw a box around each reference to **Daniel**, including pronouns.*
- *circle the word **fasting.***
- *underline every reference to **God's people**, watching carefully for pronouns and synonyms.*

DANIEL 9:1–5

1 In the first year of Darius the son of Ahasuerus, of Median descent, who was made king over the kingdom of the Chaldeans—

2 in the first year of his reign, I, Daniel, observed in the books the number of the years which was revealed as the word of the LORD to Jeremiah the prophet for the completion of the desolations of Jerusalem, namely, seventy years.

3 So I gave my attention to the Lord God to seek Him by prayer and supplications, with fasting, sackcloth and ashes.

⁴ I prayed to the LORD my God and confessed and said, "Alas, O Lord, the great and awesome God, who keeps His covenant and lovingkindness for those who love Him and keep His commandments,

⁵ we have sinned, committed iniquity, acted wickedly and rebelled, even turning aside from Your commandments and ordinances."

INSIGHT

Prayer in this passage is translated from the Hebrew word *tephillah*, which means "a plea or request of God."

Supplication is translated from the Hebrew word *tachanun*, which describes how an inferior with a need would make his request to a superior who has what is needed. The superior's granting of the request is a heartfelt response of grace.

DISCUSS

• What did you learn from marking the references to Daniel?

• Why did Daniel approach God in this way? What had Israel done?

INSIGHT

Sin is the translation of the Hebrew word *chatah,* which means "to miss the mark, to fail to meet God's standard."

Iniquity is the translation of the Hebrew word *avah,* which implies twisting or perverting God's standard.

• What disciplines accompany fasting in this passage?

• What do you think sackcloth and ashes demonstrate?

• What did you learn about how to approach God on behalf of the sin of a nation?

NEHEMIAH 1:1–11

¹ The words of Nehemiah the son of Hacaliah. Now it happened in the month Chislev, in the twentieth year, while I was in Susa the capitol,

² that Hanani, one of my brothers, and some men from Judah came; and I asked them concerning the Jews who had escaped and had survived the captivity, and about Jerusalem.

³ They said to me, "The remnant there in the province who survived the captivity are in great distress and reproach, and the wall of Jerusalem is broken down and its gates are burned with fire."

OBSERVE

Leader: Read Nehemiah 1:1–11 aloud. Have the group do the following:

- *draw a box around every reference to Nehemiah, including pronouns and synonyms such as your servant.*
- *underline each reference to the Jews, including synonyms such as the remnant and the sons of Israel.*
- *circle the word fasting.*

INSIGHT

The phrase *the twentieth year* refers to the twentieth year of the reign of King Artaxerxes of Persia, or 445 BC, ninety years after the first exiles, also called the remnant, had returned from captivity in Babylon.

The month Chislev corresponds to our November–December.

DISCUSS

• What did you learn from marking the references to Nehemiah? (Try asking the "five Ws and an H"—who, what, when, where, why, and how—to see what the text tells you about his actions in this passage.) *Who* did Nehemiah encounter in this passage? *What* was he doing? *Why* was he doing it?

• What did you learn from marking the references to the Jews, the remnant?

4 When I heard these words, I sat down and wept and mourned for days; and I was fasting and praying before the God of heaven.

5 I said, "I beseech You, O LORD God of heaven, the great and awesome God, who preserves the covenant and lovingkindness for those who love Him and keep His commandments,

6 let Your ear now be attentive and Your eyes open to hear the prayer of Your servant which I am praying before You now, day and night, on behalf of the sons of Israel Your servants, confessing the sins of the sons of

Israel which we have sinned against You; I and my father's house have sinned.

7 "We have acted very corruptly against You and have not kept the commandments, nor the statutes, nor the ordinances which You commanded Your servant Moses.

8 "Remember the word which You commanded Your servant Moses, saying, 'If you are unfaithful I will scatter you among the peoples;

9 but if you return to Me and keep My commandments and do them, though those of you who have been scattered were in the most remote part of

• What actions accompanied Nehemiah's fasting?

• What relationship do you find between sin and the fasting and prayer of Nehemiah?

• Compare Nehemiah's attitude and behavior with Daniel's in the previous passage. What do you notice?

• Summarize all you've learned about fasting, particularly what makes it more than a religious ritual.

the heavens, I will gather them from there and will bring them to the place where I have chosen to cause My name to dwell.'

10 "They are Your servants and Your people whom You redeemed by Your great power and by Your strong hand.

11 "O Lord, I beseech You, may Your ear be attentive to the prayer of Your servant and the prayer of Your servants who delight to revere Your name, and make Your servant successful today and grant him compassion before this man." Now I was the cupbearer to the king.

WRAP IT UP

Last week we learned that fasting not only involves the voluntary denial of food but also serves as a sign of humility, of contrition, of bowing low before God. This week, we saw Moses, Samuel, Daniel, and Nehemiah go before the Lord on behalf of the nation, because of the sin of their people. They prayed that the Lord might hear and respond favorably, and their prayers were accompanied by fasting and other actions: wearing sackcloth and ashes, presenting offerings, mourning, weeping, and confessing sin.

Daniel and Nehemiah included themselves in their confession of national sin, even though it is likely that they personally had not participated in the acts of unfaithfulness. But in seeking God's favor, they did not stand aloof or consider themselves superior to their fellow Jews. Instead, they confessed to being sinners in need of God's compassion, and they humbled themselves on behalf of the nation.

Where are the leaders of today, the modern-day counterparts of Samuel and Moses, who would call their organizations, their churches, their nations to repentance before God? And where are the Daniels and Nehemiahs who will come before God on their own to plead for His compassion and forgiveness on behalf of themselves and those they love?

Will you be one who draws near to God's heart by fasting, repenting, and seeking His compassion for your family, your church, your ministry, your community, your nation? We urge you to seriously consider what could happen if you were willing to do so.

So far we have seen that fasting, when accompanied by sincere confession and repentance, is an act of humility that pleases God and leads to restored fellowship. However, confession of sin is not the only reason to fast, to cry out to God. Fasting also is an appropriate response when we face circumstances beyond our power and control. This week we'll look at examples of how fasting can play a vital role when we approach God with humble petition and supplication, to seek His intervention or His direction.

OBSERVE

Jehoshaphat was king of Judah, the southern kingdom in the era of the divided kingdoms.

Leader: Read 2 Chronicles 20:1–4, 13–17 aloud. Have the group do the following:

- *draw a box around every reference to* **Jehoshaphat,** *including pronouns:*

- *draw an arrow through each occurrence of the phrase* **seek the Lord,** *like this:* →

- *circle the word* **fast.**

2 CHRONICLES 20:1–4, 13–17

¹ Now it came about after this that the sons of Moab and the sons of Ammon, together with some of the Meunites, came to make war against Jehoshaphat.

² Then some came and reported to Jehoshaphat, saying, "A great multitude is coming against you from beyond the sea, out of Aram and

behold, they are in Hazazon-tamar (that is Engedi)."

3 Jehoshaphat was afraid and turned his attention to seek the LORD, and proclaimed a fast throughout all Judah.

4 So Judah gathered together to seek help from the LORD; they even came from all the cities of Judah to seek the LORD....

13 All Judah was standing before the LORD, with their infants, their wives and their children.

14 Then in the midst of the assembly the Spirit of the LORD came upon Jahaziel the son of Zechariah, the

DISCUSS

• Summarize the situation facing Jehoshaphat and his people.

• How did Jehoshaphat handle this situation?

• What did this reveal about his personal character and his qualities as the leader of a nation? Explain your answer.

• According to verse 14 the Spirit of the Lord came upon Jahaziel and spoke to all Judah and to King Jehoshaphat. What were God's specific instructions in verses 15–17?

• What did God promise would happen if they obeyed His instructions, according to verse 17?

son of Benaiah, the son of Jeiel, the son of Mattaniah, the Levite of the sons of Asaph;

15 and he said, "Listen, all Judah and the inhabitants of Jerusalem and King Jehoshaphat: thus says the LORD to you, 'Do not fear or be dismayed because of this great multitude, for the battle is not yours but God's.

16 'Tomorrow go down against them. Behold, they will come up by the ascent of Ziz, and you will find them at the end of the valley in front of the wilderness of Jeruel.

17 'You need not fight in this battle; station yourselves, stand and see the salvation

of the LORD on your behalf, O Judah and Jerusalem.' Do not fear or be dismayed; tomorrow go out to face them, for the LORD is with you."

• Think back to a time when you found yourself in a frightening or seemingly impossible position. Did you think about fasting? Why or why not?

2 CHRONICLES 20:18–22

18 Jehoshaphat bowed his head with his face to the ground, and all Judah and the inhabitants of Jerusalem fell down before the LORD, worshiping the LORD.

19 The Levites, from the sons of the Kohathites and of the sons of the Korahites, stood up to praise the LORD God of Israel, with a very loud voice.

20 They rose early in the morning and went

OBSERVE

Leader: Read aloud 2 Chronicles 20:18–22 and have the group…

• *draw a box around every reference to* **Jehoshaphat,** *including pronouns.*
• *mark each reference to **the Lord,** including pronouns, with a triangle:* △

DISCUSS

• After the people fasted to seek help from the Lord, He spoke to them through Jahaziel. How did Jehoshaphat and the people respond upon hearing from God, according to verses 18 and 19?

• According to verse 20, what were Jehoshaphat's instructions to the people? What would be the result if they obeyed?

• What were they instructed to do in verse 21 and what was the result?

• Discuss how this relates to all we have seen in this passage so far and how it relates to Jehoshaphat calling the nation to fast.

out to the wilderness of Tekoa; and when they went out, Jehoshaphat stood and said, "Listen to me, O Judah and inhabitants of Jerusalem, put your trust in the LORD your God and you will be established. Put your trust in His prophets and succeed."

21 When he had consulted with the people, he appointed those who sang to the LORD and those who praised Him in holy attire, as they went out before the army and said, "Give thanks to the LORD, for His lovingkindness is everlasting."

22 When they began singing and praising, the LORD set ambushes

against the sons of Ammon, Moab and Mount Seir, who had come against Judah; so they were routed.

ESTHER 3:13; 4:1–3

¹³ Letters were sent by couriers to all the king's provinces to destroy, to kill and to annihilate all the Jews, both young and old, women and children, in one day, the thirteenth day of the twelfth month, which is the month Adar, and to seize their possessions as plunder....

⁴:¹ When Mordecai learned all that had been done, he tore his clothes, put on sackcloth and ashes, and went out into the midst

• What principles do you find here for trusting the Lord? What does trust look like?

OBSERVE

Mordecai was a Jew who served the king of Persia. His uncle's daughter, Esther, whom he had raised as his own, had been selected to be queen. None of the Persians knew that Esther was a Jew.

The passage we're about to read begins just after Haman, a royal advisor angered by Mordecai's refusal to bow before him, persuaded the king to issue a decree that would help him obtain his revenge.

Leader: Read Esther 3:13 and 4:1–3 aloud. As you read, have the group do the following:

- *underline every reference to **the Jews**, including pronouns.*
- *draw a box around each reference to **Mordecai**, including pronouns.*
- *circle the word **fasting**.*

DISCUSS

• Describe in detail the fate Haman had planned for the Jews in Persia and when it would occur.

• As a Jew, how did Mordecai respond to all this?

• Why were the Jews fasting and what accompanied their fasting?

INSIGHT

Sackcloth was a black cloth made of goat's hair. It was worn or laid on in mourning. Also, ashes were often sprinkled over the head or on the sackcloth as a sign of mourning.

OBSERVE

After receiving the news about Mordecai's mourning from her maidens and eunuchs, Esther sent her attendant Hathach to find out what was going on. Mordecai gave him a copy of the edict to show Esther and explained how it came about. Mordecai

of the city and wailed loudly and bitterly.

2 He went as far as the king's gate, for no one was to enter the king's gate clothed in sackcloth.

3 In each and every province where the command and decree of the king came, there was great mourning among the Jews, with fasting, weeping and wailing; and many lay on sackcloth and ashes.

ESTHER 4:13–5:3

13 Then Mordecai told them to reply to Esther, "Do not imagine that you in the king's palace can escape any more than all the Jews.

14 "For if you remain silent at this time, relief and deliverance will arise for the Jews from another place and you and your father's house will perish. And who knows whether you have not attained royalty for such a time as this?"

15 Then Esther told them to reply to Mordecai,

16 "Go, assemble all the Jews who are found in Susa, and fast for me; do not eat or drink for three days, night or day. I and my maidens also will fast in the same way. And thus I will go in to the king, which is not according to the law; and if I perish, I perish."

urged that Esther go to the king on behalf of her people. Without the king's intervention, Esther, Mordecai, and all their people would be annihilated. The problem was that Esther had not been summoned by the king for thirty days, and the law prohibited anyone from approaching the king without an invitation, on penalty of death.

Leader: Read aloud Esther 4:13–5:3 and have the group do the following:
- *mark every reference to **Esther**, including pronouns, with a big **E**.*
- *draw a box around every reference to **Mordecai**, including pronouns.*
- *circle each reference to **fasting**, watching carefully for synonymous phrases.*

DISCUSS

• Summarize Mordecai's message to Esther.

• What was Esther's response to him?

• Try asking the "five Ws and an H"—who, what, when, where, why, and how—to see what you can learn about fasting in this passage. *Who* fasted? *Why* did they fast? *How* long did they fast?

• After the period of fasting, Esther was ready to go to the king with her request. How did the king respond?

INSIGHT

Ultimately Mordecai was given a position of authority. He used that position to do the will of God, and the Jews defeated their enemies. Mordecai and Esther established the Feast of Purim, a two-day commemoration of the goodness of the Lord, who worked through circumstances to protect His people from annihilation even while they were in exile. Mordecai wrote a proclamation that the Jews were to celebrate this event annually with rejoicing, eating and giving food, and sharing with the poor.

17 So Mordecai went away and did just as Esther had commanded him.

5:1 Now it came about on the third day that Esther put on her royal robes and stood in the inner court of the king's palace in front of the king's rooms, and the king was sitting on his royal throne in the throne room, opposite the entrance to the palace.

2 When the king saw Esther the queen standing in the court, she obtained favor in his sight; and the king extended to Esther the golden scepter which was in his hand. So Esther came near and touched the top of the scepter.

³ Then the king said to her, "What is troubling you, Queen Esther? And what is your request? Even to half of the kingdom it shall be given to you."

• Have you ever witnessed an occasion when fasting was followed by clear evidence of God's gracious response?

Leader: Invite someone from the group to share a testimony about the outcome of a personal or corporate fast.

Ezra 8:21–23, 31

²¹ Then I [Ezra] proclaimed a fast there at the river of Ahava, that we might humble ourselves before our God to seek from Him a safe journey for us, our little ones, and all our possessions.

²² For I was ashamed to request from the king troops and horsemen to protect us from the enemy on the way, because we had said to the king, "The

OBSERVE

Ezra was a priest and scribe who set forth from Babylon to lead a group of Jews back to Judah after the seventy-year captivity.

Leader: Read Ezra 8:21–23, 31 aloud. As you read, have the group…
  • *draw a box around every reference to **Ezra,** including pronouns.*
  • *circle each reference to **fasting.***
  • *draw an arrow through each reference to **seeking the Lord.***

DISCUSS

• Discuss what you learned from marking the references to Ezra. Describe what was happening.

- What was Ezra's purpose for calling a fast?

- What happened as a result of the people fasting and seeking the Lord?

- What have you learned this week about fasting? In what different circumstances was fasting used to seek God's help or guidance?

hand of our God is favorably disposed to all those who seek Him, but His power and His anger are against all those who forsake Him."

23 So we fasted and sought our God concerning this matter, and He listened to our entreaty....

31 Then we journeyed from the river Ahava on the twelfth of the first month to go to Jerusalem; and the hand of our God was over us, and He delivered us from the hand of the enemy and the ambushes by the way.

WRAP IT UP

As we saw this week, fasting is not only for confession and repentance of sin but also is an appropriate action for when we face situations outside of our power and control, things that we cannot accomplish but God can. We ask God because He is God.

What are you facing today that appears to be an impossible situation?

Perhaps you, like Esther, have been drawn into a conflict between right and wrong, and taking a stand will place you at great personal risk.

Maybe your family is confronting a dire situation over which you have no control.

Has an enemy—spiritual or physical—come against you, and you don't know what to do?

Are you or someone you love threatened by disease, financial disaster, a crumbling marriage, unemployment?

When your world is coming apart and it seems that all hope is gone, do you take matters into your own hands and desperately try to figure out how to make it work? Or do you have the faith to humble yourself through fasting and seek the face of God, wait, hear from Him, and walk in obedience?

Sometimes when a leader in Israel called for a fast, the Bible describes a solemn assembly. In other words, because there was a common interest or issue, and a shared belief that they could entreat God and He would hear, the people assembled together to fast.

Let's look at the biblical record this week to see what we can discern about solemn assemblies and fasting.

OBSERVE

The prophet Joel addressed the people of Judah following a locust plague that had devastated their land. Let's observe how he challenged them to respond.

Leader: Read Joel 1:13–15 aloud. As you read, have the group do the following:
  • *underline each reference to **priests** or **ministers,** including pronouns.*
  • *circle the word* **fast.**
  • *double underline the phrase **solemn assembly.***

DISCUSS

• What were the priests told to do?

• Why were they to do it?

JOEL 1:13–15

13 Gird yourselves with sackcloth and lament, O priests; wail, O ministers of the altar! Come, spend the night in sackcloth, O ministers of my God, for the grain offering and the drink offering are withheld from the house of your God.

14 Consecrate a fast, proclaim a solemn assembly; gather the elders and all the inhabitants of the land to the house of the

LORD your God, and cry out to the LORD.

15 Alas for the day! For the day of the LORD is near, and it will come as destruction from the Almighty.

INSIGHT

The Law required a solemn assembly on the seventh day of the Feast of Unleavened Bread and the eighth day of the Feast of Tabernacles. Solemn assemblies were not required for other occasions but could be called for as needed.

• What did you observe in verse 14 about a solemn assembly? Answer as many of the "five Ws and an H"—who, what, when, where, why, and how—as you can.

JOEL 2:1, 12–17

1 Blow a trumpet in Zion, and sound an alarm on My holy mountain! Let all the inhabitants of the land tremble, for the day of the LORD is coming; surely it is near,...

12 "Yet even now," declares the LORD,

OBSERVE

Leader: *Read the selected verses from Joel aloud. Have the group...*
- *mark every reference to **the Lord**, including pronouns, with a triangle:* △
- *circle each reference to **fasting**.*
- *double underline the phrase **solemn assembly**.*

DISCUSS

• What did you learn from marking the references to the Lord? What did you learn about God's character?

• What was He telling the people to do?

• What was He telling the priests to do, and why?

"return to Me with all your heart, and with fasting, weeping and mourning;

13 and rend your heart and not your garments." Now return to the LORD your God, for He is gracious and compassionate, slow to anger, abounding in lovingkindness and relenting of evil.

14 Who knows whether He will not turn and relent and leave a blessing behind Him, even a grain offering and a drink offering for the LORD your God?

15 Blow a trumpet in Zion, consecrate a fast, proclaim a solemn assembly,

16 gather the people, sanctify the congregation, assemble the elders, gather the children and the nursing infants. Let the bridegroom come out of his room and the bride out of her bridal chamber.

17 Let the priests, the LORD'S ministers, weep between the porch and the altar, and let them say, "Spare Your people, O LORD, and do not make Your inheritance a reproach, a byword among the nations. Why should they among the peoples say, 'Where is their God?' "

• What did you learn from marking *fast*?

• *Who* should be gathered or assembled? *What* kinds of activity were to accompany the solemn assembly? *Why* were they to assemble?

OBSERVE

Amos prophesied to the northern kingdom, Israel, during a time of prosperity. Let's look at what God said through His prophet about the people's behavior during this time of richness and how it affected their relationship with Him.

Leader: *Read aloud the selected verses of Amos 5. Have the group...*

- *draw a triangle over every each occurrence of the pronouns I and Me. They refer to God, who is speaking in this passage.*
- *double underline the phrase solemn assemblies.*

DISCUSS

- What did you learn from marking the references to God?

- What did you learn about solemn assemblies?

AMOS 5:11–12, 21–24

11 ...you impose heavy rent on the poor and exact a tribute of grain from them,...

12 For I know your transgressions are many and your sins are great, you who distress the righteous and accept bribes and turn aside the poor in the gate....

21 I hate, I reject your festivals, nor do I delight in your solemn assemblies.

22 Even though you offer up to Me burnt offerings and your grain offerings, I will not accept them; and I will not even look at the peace offerings of your fatlings.

23 Take away from Me the noise of your songs; I will not even listen to the sound of your harps.

24 But let justice roll down like waters and righteousness like an ever-flowing stream.

• How does verse 24 explain what God said in verses 21–23?

ISAIAH 1:2–4, 11–15

2 Listen, O heavens, and hear, O earth; for the LORD speaks, "Sons I have reared and brought up, but they have revolted against Me.

3 "An ox knows its owner, and a donkey its master's manger, but Israel does not know, My people do not understand."

OBSERVE

Isaiah warned the southern kingdom of Judah about the judgment to come because of her sin, rebellion, and idolatry. Let's look at how God felt about her attitude toward Him.

Leader: Read the selected verses from Isaiah aloud and have the group...
- *underline each reference to **the people of Israel**, including pronouns and synonyms.*
- *mark a slash like this ╱ through each reference to **sin**, watching carefully for synonyms such as **act corruptly** and **iniquity**.*

• *double underline the phrases **calling of assemblies** and **solemn assembly.***

DISCUSS

• What did you learn from marking the references to the people? Describe their relationship to God during this time.

• How did God feel about their solemn assemblies, and why?

⁴ Alas, sinful nation, people weighed down with iniquity, offspring of evildoers, sons who act corruptly! They have abandoned the LORD, they have despised the Holy One of Israel, they have turned away from Him....

¹¹ "What are your multiplied sacrifices to Me?" says the LORD. "I have had enough of burnt offerings of rams and the fat of fed cattle; and I take no pleasure in the blood of bulls, lambs or goats.

¹² "When you [Judah] come to appear before Me, who requires of you this trampling of My courts?

13 "Bring your worthless offerings no longer, incense is an abomination to Me. New moon and sabbath, the calling of assemblies—I cannot endure iniquity and the solemn assembly.

14 "I hate your new moon festivals and your appointed feasts, they have become a burden to Me; I am weary of bearing them.

15 "So when you spread out your hands in prayer, I will hide My eyes from you; yes, even though you multiply prayers, I will not listen. Your hands are covered with blood."

• Do you see any relationship between the state of a man's heart and his performance of religious rituals?

OBSERVE

You probably remember the story of Jonah defying God's instructions to go to Nineveh, and consequently finding himself in the belly of a great fish. After Jonah repented of his willful disobedience, God again sent him to Nineveh to call the city to repentance. Let's see how the people responded to his message.

Leader: Read Jonah 3 aloud. As you read, have the group do the following:
- *circle the word **fast** and **any synonyms for fasting.***
- *draw an arrow through the phrase **call on God**, like this:* ⟶
- *draw a mark like this* ⟋⟍ *over the words **turn** and **turned from.***

DISCUSS

- Discuss the events of this chapter. What was happening?

JONAH 3

1 Now the word of the LORD came to Jonah the second time, saying,

2 "Arise, go to Nineveh the great city and proclaim to it the proclamation which I am going to tell you."

3 So Jonah arose and went to Nineveh according to the word of the LORD. Now Nineveh was an exceedingly great city, a three days' walk.

4 Then Jonah began to go through the city one day's walk; and he cried out and said, "Yet forty days and Nineveh will be overthrown."

5 Then the people of Nineveh believed in God; and they called a fast and put on sackcloth from the greatest to the least of them.

6 When the word reached the king of Nineveh, he arose from his throne, laid aside his robe from him, covered himself with sackcloth and sat on the ashes.

7 He issued a proclamation and it said, "In Nineveh by the decree of the king and his nobles: Do not let man, beast, herd, or flock taste a thing. Do not let them eat or drink water.

8 "But both man and beast must be

• Why did the people of Nineveh fast?

• What else did the people of Nineveh do besides fast?

• When Jonah preached the message God gave him for Nineveh, the people mourned over their sin, fasted, and repented. Although the phrase "solemn assembly" is not used in this passage, in essence the gentile king called for a solemn assembly when he heard the prophet's message. The result was that God did not bring calamity on them. How does this compare to what Amos, Joel, and Isaiah preached, and what did you learn about God from these passages?

covered with sack-cloth; and let men call on God earnestly that each may turn from his wicked way and from the violence which is in his hands.

9 "Who knows, God may turn and relent and withdraw His burning anger so that we will not perish."

10 When God saw their deeds, that they turned from their wicked way, then God relented concerning the calamity which He had declared He would bring upon them. And He did not do it.

WRAP IT UP

The Law required Israel to hold solemn assemblies at the end of the feasts of Unleavened Bread and Tabernacles, but these were not fast days. The Law only required a fast on the Day of Atonement.

When Israel assembled together for what are called "solemn assemblies" apart from the feasts, it was for special occasions, times of national or corporate need, when they came to entreat God. In Israel's case, the national and religious entreaties to God were often the same, since Israel was a theocracy, ruled by God, and sin was the core issue. The prophets had warned Israel that God was not pleased with His people. Although they continued performing their religious rituals, as a nation they were tolerating iniquity and had rejected righteousness and justice.

Solemn assemblies were called to show Israel that their sin was common, not private. An assembly of persons creates a greater awareness of the dimensions of the crisis. The hope was that exposing the depth of corporate depravity—and the shallowness of their religious activity—would prompt corporate repentance and a return to God.

Today when we think of corporate need, we can think of the church, under God's rule. Rather than looking down on Israel in judgment, perhaps we should confess the sins of the "worshiping church." Nearly every household in the United States has a Bible, there are plenty of churches, and an overwhelming majority of people claim to be religious. What impact does all this "religion" have on the culture today? Divorce, immorality, and crime rates are soaring both inside and outside the church.

Perhaps, like the worshipers in the days of the prophets, we are merely going through the motions. Could it be that many of us are so religious we don't see the need to repent? What do you think would be the result if churches held solemn assemblies and truly evaluated their worship and their lifestyles? Would the people see the need to repent and return to God?

Why do we so often see prayer paired with fasting in the Scriptures? Fasting should be done in the context of prayer as a means of communicating with God at a deep heart level. This week let's consider what such prayer should look like and what the result will be.

OBSERVE

We are going to look at a number of New Testament passages to see what we can learn in general terms about the purpose of prayer and how it should be done.

Leader: Read aloud the selected verses from 1 Timothy 2.
   • *As you read, have the group mark each reference to **prayer**, including synonyms such as **entreaties** and **petitions**, with a big **P**.*

DISCUSS

• According to this passage, who is to pray?

• Who are they to pray for?

• What is to accompany these prayers?

1 Timothy 2:1–4, 8

¹ First of all, then, I urge that entreaties and prayers, petitions and thanksgivings, be made on behalf of all men,

² for kings and all who are in authority, so that we may lead a tranquil and quiet life in all godliness and dignity.

³ This is good and acceptable in the sight of God our Savior,

⁴ who desires all men to be saved and to come to the knowledge of the truth....

8 Therefore I want the men in every place to pray, lifting up holy hands, without wrath and dissension.

• Why are they to pray?

• How are they to pray?

INSIGHT

Entreaty is translated from the Greek word *deesis,* which means "to ask for something which is lacking and which is needed."

Petition is translated from the Greek word *enteuxis,* which refers to conversing with or addressing someone. The word implies freedom of access and boldness in coming to God. It sometimes means "intercession."

PHILIPPIANS 4:6–7

6 Be anxious for nothing, but in everything by prayer and supplication with thanksgiving let your requests be made known to God.

OBSERVE

Leader: *Read Philippians 4:6–7 aloud.*
  • *Have the group mark every reference to* **prayer,** *including synonyms, with a* **P.**

DISCUSS

• What commands are given in these verses?

INSIGHT

Supplication is translated from the Greek word *deesis*. The same word is translated as "entreaty" in 1 Timothy 2:1. It means "to ask for something which is lacking and which is needed."

7 And the peace of God, which surpasses all comprehension, will guard your hearts and your minds in Christ Jesus.

• What is the benefit of obeying these commands?

• From what you read in these verses and in the Insight box, discuss how following these instructions would affect your life.

OBSERVE

In his letter to the believers in Ephesus, Paul discussed the issue of spiritual warfare and followed this by emphasizing the importance of prayer.

Leader: Read Ephesians 6:18–19 aloud.
• *As you do, have the group mark the words **prayer, petition,** and **pray** with a* **P.**

EPHESIANS 6:18–19

18 With all prayer and petition pray at all times in the Spirit, and with this in view, be on the alert with all perseverance and petition for all the saints,

19 and pray on my behalf, that utterance may be given to me in the opening of my mouth, to make known with boldness the mystery of the gospel.

DISCUSS

• Keeping in mind the spiritual battle we are in, what did you learn about prayer in these verses?

• In verse 18 Paul urged believers to pray for the saints in this time of war. Discuss how we are to pray and what this would look like practically.

• This kind of praying is called intercession. Have someone in your group describe a time when they interceded in prayer for others.

1 THESSALONIANS 5:16–18

16 Rejoice always;

17 pray without ceasing;

18 in everything give thanks; for this is God's will for you in Christ Jesus.

OBSERVE

Leader: Read aloud 1 Thessalonians 5:16–18.

> • *Have the group mark the word **pray** with a **P.***

DISCUSS

• How are we to pray? Discuss what that would look like in your daily life.

• Now let's review. What have we learned so far about prayer? Who is to pray? When? Why? How? What are they to pray for?

OBSERVE

Now let's turn our attention to some passages that join fasting with prayer. First we'll look at the description of a faithful woman who was present when Mary and Joseph brought Jesus to the temple to present Him to the Lord.

Leader: Read Luke 2:36–38 aloud. As you read, have the group do the following:
  • *draw a box around each reference to Anna, including pronouns.*
  • *circle the word **fastings.***
  • *mark the word **prayers** with a* **P.**

DISCUSS

• What did you learn about Anna?

LUKE 2:36–38

36 And there was a prophetess, Anna the daughter of Phanuel, of the tribe of Asher. She was advanced in years and had lived with her husband seven years after her marriage,

37 and then as a widow to the age of eighty-four. She never left the temple, serving night and day with fastings and prayers.

38 At that very moment she came up and began giving thanks to God, and continued to speak of Him to all those who were looking for the redemption of Jerusalem.

ACTS 13:1–3

¹ Now there were at Antioch, in the church that was there, prophets and teachers: Barnabas, and Simeon who was called Niger, and Lucius of Cyrene, and Manaen who had been brought up with Herod the tetrarch, and Saul.

² While they were ministering to the Lord and fasting, the Holy Spirit said, "Set apart for Me Barnabas and Saul for the work to which I have called them."

• What role did fasting and prayer play in her life?

• How did God bless her service to Him?

OBSERVE

Leader: *Read Acts 13:1–3 aloud. Have the group…*

- *underline every reference to **prophets and teachers,** including the pronouns **they, them,** and **their.***
- *circle the word **fasted.***
- *mark the word **prayed** with a* **P.**

INSIGHT

The phrase *ministering to the Lord* is translated from the Greek word *leitourgeo,* from which we get our English word *liturgy.* It refers to service to God.

The act of laying hands on a person identified the church with that individual's ministry and acknowledged God's direction in his or her life.

DISCUSS

• Who fasted in this passage?

• What did the Holy Spirit direct them to do while they were worshiping and fasting, according to verse 2?

• After they had fasted and prayed, what did these men do, and what did it signify?

OBSERVE

Leader: *Read Acts 14:21–23 aloud. As you read, have the group…*
- *draw a box around each reference to* **Paul and Barnabas,** *including the pronouns* **they** *and* **we.**
- *mark the word* **prayed** *with a* **P.**
- *circle the word* **fasting.**

DISCUSS

• What was the occasion or purpose for prayer and fasting in this passage?

• How does this passage relate to what you read in Acts 13:1–3?

3 Then, when they had fasted and prayed and laid their hands on them, they sent them away.

ACTS 14:21–23

21 After they [Paul and Barnabas] had preached the gospel to that city and had made many disciples, they returned to Lystra and to Iconium and to Antioch,

22 strengthening the souls of the disciples, encouraging them to continue in the faith, and saying, "Through many tribulations we must enter the kingdom of God."

23 When they had appointed elders for them in every church, having prayed with fasting, they commended them to the Lord in whom they had believed.

• What do Acts 13 and 14 indicate about ministry in the early church? What relevance could this have for believers today?

PSALM 69:1–4, 10–13

1 Save me [David], O God, for the waters have threatened my life.

2 I have sunk in deep mire, and there is no foothold; I have come into deep waters, and a flood overflows me.

3 I am weary with my crying; my throat is parched; my eyes fail while I wait for my God.

4 Those who hate me without a cause are

OBSERVE

Let's look at one more passage, in which we see the psalmist David pouring out his heart to God in prayer.

Leader: *Read the selected verses from Psalm 69 aloud. As you read, have the group…*
  * *mark every reference to **David,** including the pronouns **I** and **me,** with a big **D.***
  * *circle the word **fasting.***
  * *mark the word **prayer** with a **P.***

DISCUSS

• What were David's circumstances?

• What did he do in his sorrow?

• How did others respond to David's prayer and fasting?

• Did that stop him? Explain your answer.

• How important was prayer and fasting to David? How important is it to you?

more than the hairs of my head; those who would destroy me are powerful, being wrongfully my enemies; what I did not steal, I then have to restore....

10 When I wept in my soul with fasting, it became my reproach.

11 When I made sackcloth my clothing, I became a byword to them.

12 Those who sit in the gate talk about me, and I am the song of the drunkards.

13 But as for me, my prayer is to You, O LORD, at an acceptable time; O God, in the greatness of Your lovingkindness, answer me with Your saving truth.

WRAP IT UP

Prayer and fasting are both humble offerings to the Lord. We see prayer as incense offered up to God in both the Old and New Testaments:

O LORD, I call upon You; hasten to me!

Give ear to my voice when I call to You!

May my prayer be counted as incense before You;

The lifting up of my hands as the evening offering. (Psalm 141:1–2)

Another angel came and stood at the altar, holding a golden censer; and much incense was given to him, so that he might add it to the prayers of all the saints on the golden altar which was before the throne. And the smoke of the incense, with the prayers of the saints, went up before God out of the angel's hand. (Revelation 8:3–4)

As we have seen, God cares deeply about the attitude in which prayer and fasting are offered. As the apostle Paul noted, "Whatever is not from faith is sin" (Romans 14:23).

What about you? Is your fasting done in the context of prayer? Are you too self-sufficient and too proud to pray to the God who made you? Or are you willing to humble yourself and fast and pray in faith as part of your spiritual growth?[1]

---

[1] To learn more about the power of prayer in your daily life, we recommend the 40-Minute study *The Essentials of Effective Prayer*.

During the past five weeks, we've seen principles from the Bible about entering into fasting and prayer as part of confessing sin, both personal and corporate, and as a means of seeking God's favor and direction. This week we'll apply what we've learned. As we pore over the Scriptures, let's examine our hearts and seek the Lord today on behalf of ourselves, our families, our churches, our communities, and our nation.

We'll start by looking at passages that might direct and assist us in our prayers, confessions, supplications, and intercessions on behalf of our nation. As you know, because God is holy, He cannot overlook sin. Sin must be recognized as sin, repented of, confessed, and forsaken—or it must be judged.

OBSERVE

In the following passage we read the prophet Ezekiel's declaration to the city of Jerusalem, making it clear that her days are numbered because her crimes demand punishment.

Leader: *Read Ezekiel 22:1–11 aloud. As you read, have the group…*

* *underline references to **the bloody city**, including any synonyms and pronouns such as **her, you,** and **they** when they refer to the city or its inhabitants.*

EZEKIEL 22:1–11

1 Then the word of the LORD came to me, saying,

2 "And you, son of man, will you judge, will you judge the bloody city? Then cause her to know all her abominations.

3 "You shall say, 'Thus says the LORD God, "A city shedding

blood in her midst, so that her time will come, and that makes idols, contrary to her interest, for defilement!

4 "You have become guilty by the blood which you have shed, and defiled by your idols which you have made. Thus you have brought your day near and have come to your years; therefore I have made you a reproach to the nations and a mocking to all the lands.

5 "Those who are near and those who are far from you will mock you, you of ill repute, full of turmoil.

6 "Behold, the rulers of Israel, each according to his power, have been in you for the

• *place a check mark like this ✓ over each of **the sins committed by the people of the city.***

DISCUSS

• What accusations were brought against the bloody city?

• According to verse 4, what was the verdict, and why?

• What was the result of this verdict?

purpose of shedding blood.

7 "They have treated father and mother lightly within you. The alien they have oppressed in your midst; the fatherless and the widow they have wronged in you.

8 "You have despised My holy things and profaned My sabbaths.

9 "Slanderous men have been in you for the purpose of shedding blood, and in you they have eaten at the mountain shrines. In your midst they have committed acts of lewdness.

10 "In you they have uncovered their fathers' nakedness; in

you they have humbled her who was unclean in her menstrual impurity.

11 "One has committed abomination with his neighbor's wife and another has lewdly defiled his daughter-in-law. And another in you has humbled his sister, his father's daughter." ' "

EZEKIEL 22:12–22

12 "In you they have taken bribes to shed blood; you have taken interest and profits, and you have injured your neighbors for gain by oppression, and you have forgotten Me," declares the Lord GOD.

13 "Behold, then, I smite My hand at your dishonest gain which

• Look back at each of the sins you checked and discuss whether or not America is guilty of the same thing. Explain your answers.

OBSERVE

Leader: Read aloud Ezekiel 22:12–22 and have the group do the following:

- *underline each **you** and **they** that refers to **the people of Jerusalem.***
- *place a check mark over **each sinful act the people are committing.***
- *mark every reference to **the Lord**, including pronouns, with a triangle:* △

DISCUSS

• What, if anything, did you learn from marking the references to the people of Jerusalem?

• What did you learn from marking the references to God? What did God say He was preparing to do?

you have acquired and at the bloodshed which is among you.

14 "Can your heart endure, or can your hands be strong in the days that I will deal with you? I, the LORD, have spoken and will act.

15 "I will scatter you among the nations and I will disperse you through the lands, and I will consume your uncleanness from you.

16 "You will profane yourself in the sight of the nations, and you will know that I am the LORD."

17 And the word of the LORD came to me, saying,

18 "Son of man, the house of Israel has

become dross to Me; all of them are bronze and tin and iron and lead in the furnace; they are the dross of silver.

19 "Therefore, thus says the Lord GOD, 'Because all of you have become dross, therefore, behold, I am going to gather you into the midst of Jerusalem.

20 'As they gather silver and bronze and iron and lead and tin into the furnace to blow fire on it in order to melt it, so I will gather you in My anger and in My wrath and I will lay you there and melt you.

21 'I will gather you and blow on you with the fire of My wrath,

• What metaphor did God use to describe what He was about to do?

INSIGHT

Silver was refined by placing it in a fire until the impurities, or dross, were released from the silver and rose to the surface. The dross was then skimmed off the melted liquid and discarded.

• According to these verses, how would God remove the impurities of the people?

and you will be melted in the midst of it.

22 'As silver is melted in the furnace, so you will be melted in the midst of it; and you will know that I, the LORD, have poured out My wrath on you.' "

OBSERVE

Leader: Read Ezekiel 22:23–31 aloud. Have the group…

- *underline every reference to **the land and its inhabitants,** including pronouns.*
- *draw a box around every reference to **the leaders,** such as **prophets, priests,** and **princes** and any corresponding pronouns.*
- *draw a triangle over every reference to **the Lord,** including pronouns.*

DISCUSS

• What did you learn from marking the references to the people of the land?

EZEKIEL 22:23–31

23 And the word of the LORD came to me, saying,

24 "Son of man, say to her, 'You are a land that is not cleansed or rained on in the day of indignation.'

25 "There is a conspiracy of her prophets in her midst like a roaring lion tearing the prey. They have devoured lives; they have taken treasure and

precious things; they have made many widows in the midst of her.

26 "Her priests have done violence to My law and have profaned My holy things; they have made no distinction between the holy and the profane, and they have not taught the difference between the unclean and the clean; and they hide their eyes from My sabbaths, and I am profaned among them.

27 "Her princes within her are like wolves tearing the prey, by shedding blood and destroying lives in order to get dishonest gain.

28 "Her prophets have smeared whitewash for

• What did you learn about the prophets? the priests? the princes?

• Discuss any parallels you see between these leaders and the type of leadership prevalent in our nation.

• What does this suggest about the kind of leadership we are to pray for?

• What did you learn from marking the references to the Lord?

them, seeing false visions and divining lies for them, saying, 'Thus says the Lord GOD,' when the LORD has not spoken.

29 "The people of the land have practiced oppression and committed robbery, and they have wronged the poor and needy and have oppressed the sojourner without justice.

30 "I searched for a man among them who would build up the wall and stand in the gap before Me for the land, so that I would not destroy it; but I found no one.

31 "Thus I have poured out My indignation on them; I have

consumed them with the fire of My wrath; their way I have brought upon their heads," declares the Lord GOD.

• How could you serve today as the man or woman God is looking for, as described in verse 30?

DANIEL 9:1–11

¹ In the first year of Darius the son of Ahasuerus, of Median descent, who was made king over the kingdom of the Chaldeans—

² in the first year of his reign, I, Daniel, observed in the books the number of the years which was revealed as the word of the LORD to Jeremiah the prophet for the completion of the desolations of Jerusalem, namely, seventy years.

OBSERVE

In lesson two we observed that Daniel's study of the Scriptures prompted a prayer of confession and petition along with his fasting. He understood that obedience would bring blessing and disobedience would bring discipline. Israel's Babylonian experience was the proof of this principle. Daniel also understood, however, that if the people would return and obey God, He would restore and bless them. Let's give further attention to his words in light of this truth.

Leader: Read aloud Daniel 9:1–11 and have the group...

• underline every reference to **the people,** including synonyms such as **men of Judah** and **all Israel,** as well as pronouns such as **we, us, our, them,** and **their.**

• *place a check mark over **every specific sin** mentioned in Daniel's prayer.*

DISCUSS

• What did you learn from marking the references to the people of Judah?

³ So I gave my attention to the Lord God to seek Him by prayer and supplications, with fasting, sackcloth and ashes.

⁴ I prayed to the LORD my God and confessed and said, "Alas, O Lord, the great and awesome God, who keeps His covenant and lovingkindness for those who love Him and keep His commandments,

⁵ we have sinned, committed iniquity, acted wickedly and rebelled, even turning aside from Your commandments and ordinances.

⁶ "Moreover, we have not listened to Your servants the prophets, who spoke

in Your name to our kings, our princes, our fathers and all the people of the land.

7 "Righteousness belongs to You, O Lord, but to us open shame, as it is this day—to the men of Judah, the inhabitants of Jerusalem and all Israel, those who are nearby and those who are far away in all the countries to which You have driven them, because of their unfaithful deeds which they have committed against You.

8 "Open shame belongs to us, O Lord, to our kings, our princes and our fathers, because we have sinned against You.

• What parallels, if any, do you see between the state of Judah then and the condition of America today? Discuss your observations.

• What was Daniel doing in this segment of chapter 9?

• Stop at this time, and in light of what you've learned from Ezekiel 22 and Daniel 9, confess the sins of our nation. At this point, do nothing else but confess the sins God lays on your heart. Your confessions need not be lengthy. Simply wait upon God, and as He brings sins to mind, confess them aloud so the group can participate in this confession.

Leader: *Allow enough time for anyone who feels led to pray aloud to do so. Keep in mind you should only confess the sins God brings to your heart.*

9 "To the Lord our God belong compassion and forgiveness, for we have rebelled against Him;

10 nor have we obeyed the voice of the LORD our God, to walk in His teachings which He set before us through His servants the prophets.

11 "Indeed all Israel has transgressed Your law and turned aside, not obeying Your voice; so the curse has been poured out on us, along with the oath which is written in the law of Moses the servant of God, for we have sinned against Him."

DANIEL 9:12–19

12 "Thus He has confirmed His words which He had spoken against us and against our rulers who ruled us, to bring on us great calamity; for under the whole heaven there has not been done anything like what was done to Jerusalem.

13 "As it is written in the law of Moses, all this calamity has come on us; yet we have not sought the favor of the LORD our God by turning from our iniquity and giving attention to Your truth.

14 "Therefore the LORD has kept the calamity in store and brought it on us; for the LORD our God is righteous with respect to all

OBSERVE

Leader: *Read Daniel 9:12–19 aloud. As you read, have the group...*

- *mark with a triangle every reference to **God,** including pronouns.*
- *mark a slash like this ⁄ through each reference to **sin,** watching carefully for synonyms such as **iniquity, wicked,** and **not obeyed.***
- *draw a cloud like this ☁ around every reference to calamity and wrath.*

DISCUSS

- What did you learn about God in verse 12?

- What did you learn from marking *calamity* and *wrath*?

• From all you have seen, why had God brought such calamity on His people?

• Keeping all of this in mind, what did you learn about God's character?

• What did you learn about the character of His people? How does that compare with God's character?

His deeds which He has done, but we have not obeyed His voice.

15 "And now, O Lord our God, who have brought Your people out of the land of Egypt with a mighty hand and have made a name for Yourself, as it is this day—we have sinned, we have been wicked.

16 "O Lord, in accordance with all Your righteous acts, let now Your anger and Your wrath turn away from Your city Jerusalem, Your holy mountain; for because of our sins and the iniquities of our fathers, Jerusalem and Your people have become a reproach to all those around us.

17 "So now, our God, listen to the prayer of Your servant and to his supplications, and for Your sake, O Lord, let Your face shine on Your desolate sanctuary.

18 "O my God, incline Your ear and hear! Open Your eyes and see our desolations and the city which is called by Your name; for we are not presenting our supplications before You on account of any merits of our own, but on account of Your great compassion.

19 "O Lord, hear! O Lord, forgive! O Lord, listen and take action! For Your own sake, O my God, do not delay, because Your city and Your people are called by Your name."

• According to verses 17–19, what was Daniel asking? List everything he was asking God to do.

• On what basis was he asking this?

• What does this passage suggest about God's involvement in adversity? What does this insight suggest about recent events in your life? in your community? in our nation?

WRAP IT UP

Our study of the Old Testament showed that fasting was a way men might humble themselves (Ezra 8:21). It also served as a means by which to seek direction from the Lord (2 Chronicles 20:3–4). However, the prophets declared that without proper behavior a man's fasting was in vain (Isaiah 58:5–12).

We also saw in the New Testament that Jesus assumed His followers would fast; however, He taught them not to do so in order to be noticed by men. Instead, fasting is to be associated with dependence on God, sought genuinely with a pure heart. It is to be practiced joyfully and with thanksgiving as a service to God. Fasting is to be grounded in faith as a means of spiritual growth.

As we bring our study to a close, let's look at the fasting testimony of Rev. John Meador while he was pastor of Woodland Park Baptist Church in Chattanooga, Tennessee:

Facing some critical decisions in the life of our church that involved both money and people, I sensed the Lord leading me to my first forty-day fast. How can you summarize "being led" to do something like that? Only by saying it was not my idea, and that God repeatedly opened my eyes to scriptural references to the practice of fasting. I was worried I couldn't make it, concerned that I'd do it wrong, wondering how I could maintain daily life, but I could not deny God was calling me to come to Him in fasting and prayer. It was an amazing experience of dependence and listening. God used that time to break me in several ways—most notably breaking my will when it came to the decision I was facing.

It has been said that the easiest way to know the will of God is to abandon your own will, and I learned the truth of that during the fast. It seemed I was starving my body while feeding my soul in prayer and reading the Word. It also seems I was starving my own will, suffocating it, so that I might recognize God's will. I can honestly say that God spoke to me as clearly and more frequently than ever before. I was amazed at the clarity and stunned by the daily strength He gave me, in spite of eating no food for forty days. At the end of the fast, I was reluctant to eat again—it was that precious of a time with God. But I knew it was time. In the end, God's direction to me in that period formed the basis for a decision that brought unity, vision, and provision in many ways.

What about you? Knowing that Jesus expects us to fast, are you willing to walk in obedience and dependence on Him?

40 MINUTE BIBLE STUDIES

No-Homework

That Help You

A 6-WEEK, NO-HOMEWORK BIBLE STUDY
MORE THAN 700,000 SOLD IN THE SERIES

Being a Disciple:
Counting the
Real Cost

Kay Arthur, Tom & Jane Hart

PRECEPT MINISTRIES INTERNATIONAL

40minute BIBLE STUDY

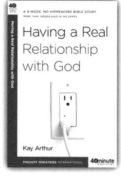

A 6-WEEK, NO-HOMEWORK BIBLE STUDY
MORE THAN 700,000 SOLD IN THE SERIES

Having a Real
Relationship
with God

Kay Arthur

PRECEPT MINISTRIES INTERNATIONAL

40minute BIBLE STUDY

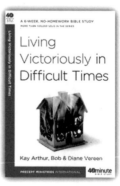

A 6-WEEK, NO-HOMEWORK BIBLE STUDY
MORE THAN 700,000 SOLD IN THE SERIES

How Do You
Walk the Walk
You Talk?

Kay Arthur

PRECEPT MINISTRIES INTERNATIONAL

40minute BIBLE STUDY

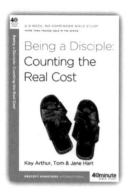

A 6-WEEK, NO-HOMEWORK BIBLE STUDY
MORE THAN 700,000 SOLD IN THE SERIES

Living a
Life of
True Worship

Kay Arthur, Bob & Diane Vereen

PRECEPT MINISTRIES INTERNATIONAL

40minute BIBLE STUDY

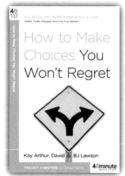

A 6-WEEK, NO-HOMEWORK BIBLE STUDY
MORE THAN 700,000 SOLD IN THE SERIES

Living
Victoriously in
Difficult Times

Kay Arthur, Bob & Diane Vereen

PRECEPT MINISTRIES INTERNATIONAL

40minute BIBLE STUDY

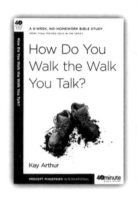

A 6-WEEK, NO-HOMEWORK BIBLE STUDY
MORE THAN 700,000 SOLD IN THE SERIES

How to Make
Choices You
Won't Regret

Kay Arthur, David & BJ Lawson

PRECEPT MINISTRIES INTERNATIONAL

40minute BIBLE STUDY

A 6-WEEK, NO-HOMEWORK BIBLE STUDY
MORE THAN 700,000 SOLD IN THE SERIES

Money and
Possessions:
The Quest for
Contentment

Kay Arthur & David Arthur

PRECEPT MINISTRIES INTERNATIONAL

40minute BIBLE STUDY

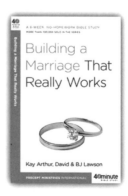

A 6-WEEK, NO-HOMEWORK BIBLE STUDY
MORE THAN 700,000 SOLD IN THE SERIES

Building a
Marriage That
Really Works

Kay Arthur, David & BJ Lawson

PRECEPT MINISTRIES INTERNATIONAL

40minute BIBLE STUDY

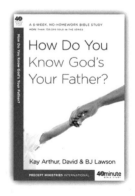

A 6-WEEK, NO-HOMEWORK BIBLE STUDY
MORE THAN 700,000 SOLD IN THE SERIES

How Do You
Know God's
Your Father?

Kay Arthur, David & BJ Lawson

PRECEPT MINISTRIES INTERNATIONAL

40minute BIBLE STUDY

Bible Studies
Discover Truth For Yourself

Discovering What the Future Holds

Kay Arthur & Georg Huber

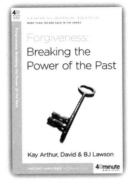

Forgiveness: Breaking the Power of the Past

Kay Arthur, David & BJ Lawson

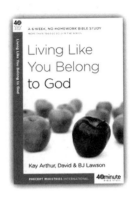

Living Like You Belong to God

Kay Arthur, David & BJ Lawson

The Essentials of Effective Prayer

Kay Arthur, David & BJ Lawson

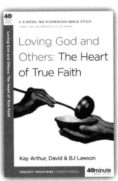

Loving God and Others: The Heart of True Faith

Kay Arthur, David & BJ Lawson

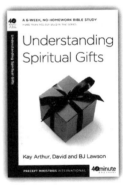

Understanding Spiritual Gifts

Kay Arthur, David and BJ Lawson

Also Available:
A Man's Strategy for Conquering Temptation
Rising to the Call of Leadership
Key Principles of Biblical Fasting
What Does the Bible Say About Sex?
Turning Your Heart Toward God
Fatal Distractions: Conquering Destructive Temptations
Spiritual Warfare: Overcoming the Enemy
The Power of Knowing God
Breaking Free from Fear

Another powerful study series
from beloved Bible teacher

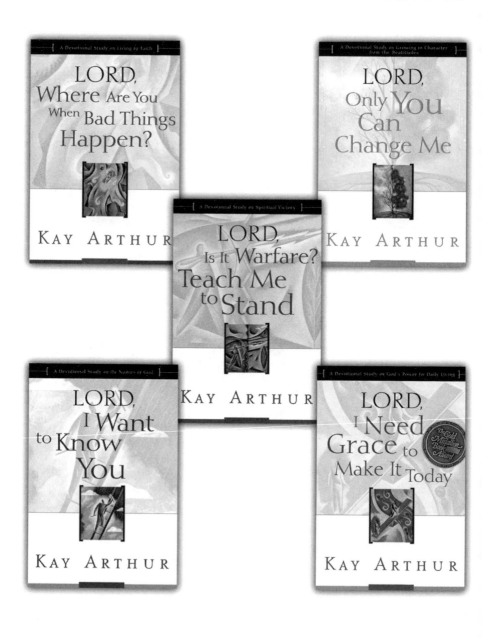

KAY ARTHUR

The Lord series provides insightful, warm-hearted Bible studies designed to meet you where you are —and help you discover God's answers to your deepest needs.

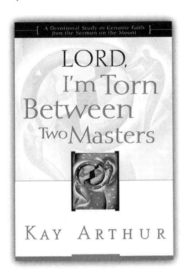

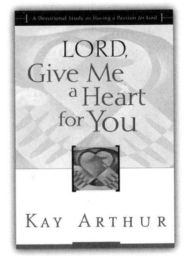

ALSO AVAILABLE:
One-year devotionals to draw you closer to the heart of God.

KAY ARTHUR is known around the world as an international Bible teacher, author, conference speaker, and host of the national radio and television programs *Precepts for Life,* which reaches a worldwide viewing audience of over 94 million. A four-time Gold Medallion Award–winning author, Kay has authored more than 100 books and Bible studies.

Kay and her husband, Jack, founded Precept Ministries International in 1970 in Chattanooga, Tennessee, with a vision to establish people in God's Word. Today, the ministry has a worldwide outreach. In addition to inductive study training workshops and thousands of small-group studies across America, PMI reaches nearly 150 countries with inductive Bible studies translated into nearly 70 languages, teaching people to discover Truth for themselves.

PETE DE LACY began leading Precept Upon Precept Bible studies and conducting training workshops in inductive study in the 1980s. He joined the staff of PMI in 1989 after retiring from a career in the U.S. Army. The author of several books in the New Inductive Study Series and the 40-Minute Bible Study series, he is a contributor to *The New Inductive Study Bible, Discover the Bible for Yourself,* and *How to Study the Bible.* Pete also is a featured teacher at Precept Ministries Conferences and in many Precept Upon Precept videos.

Contact Precept Ministries International for more information about inductive Bible studies in your area.

Precept Ministries International
P.O. Box 182218
Chattanooga, TN 37422-7218
800-763-8280
www.precept.org